Emma & Egor

Signing Exact English &
American Sign Language

First WORDS

Lilly

Max

Sam

This Book is dedicated to Alexandra:

Thank you for being my ongoing inspiration in creating
a **Signing Exact English** educational program that will positively
impact the education and development of ALL children.

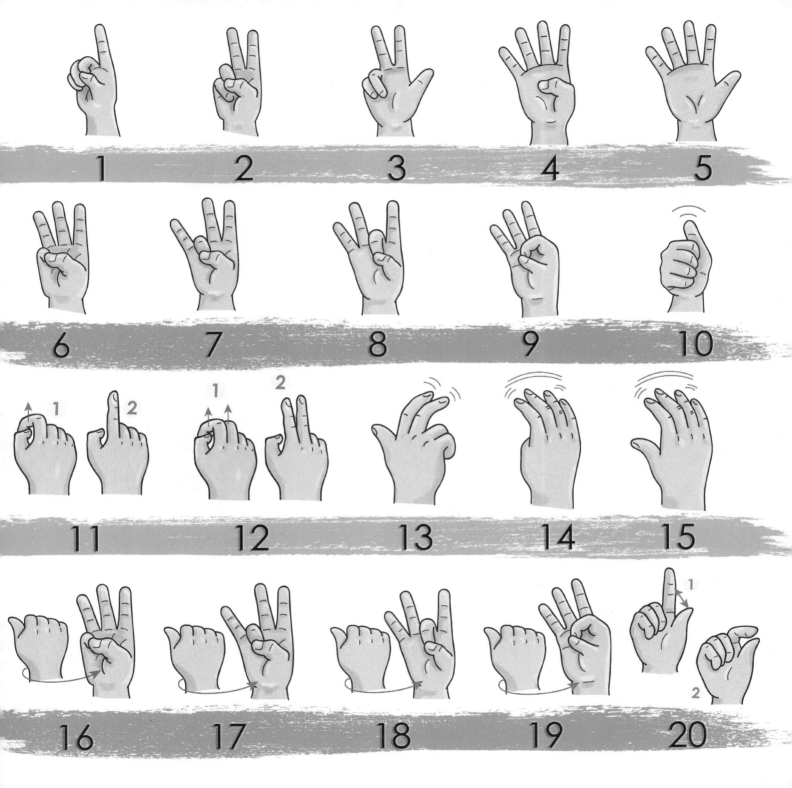

Girl

Thumb of right "A" hand moves down jawline.

Boy

1) Open right hand at forehead.
2) Fingers and thumb come together (as if grasping the brim of a hat).

Dog

Right hand at chest level, snap fingers.

Cat

Right "F" hand at edge of mouth, draws out whiskers.

"A" hands on chest, rub knuckles up and down.

Bath

Clean

Right palm wipes once over left palm.

Ball

Hands in front of the chest form the shape of a ball.

Game

2x

"A" hands thumbs up, palms in, bump knuckles together.

Grandmother Grandfather

Right hand wide open, thumb on chin moves out and away, creating two humps.

Right hand wide open, thumb on forehead moves out and away, creating two humps.

Friend

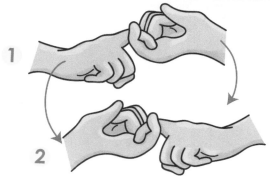

Index fingers hook together,
first right over left,
then left over right.

Hot

1) "C" hand at mouth, palm in.
2) Twist wrist out and down.

Cold

"S" hands in front of chest, shake as if shivering.

Truck

"T" hands face in, right hand
rests on thumb of left hand.
Lift and lower right hand.

Car

ASL sign

"C" hands face in, right hand
rests on thumb of left hand.
Lift and lower right hand.

"S" hands at chest level
move as if driving a car.

Share

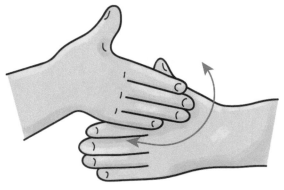

Left hand at chest level, palm open. Right hand, palm open, little finger slides back and forth between left index finger and thumb.

Yucky

Flick right middle finger
off of the thumb twice.

Breakfast

ASL sign

Right "B" hand moves in a circular motion at corner of mouth.

1) Right "O" hand makes eating motion in front of mouth.
2) Left "B" hand, palm in rests on inside of right forearm.
Right "B" hand, palm in rises (as if sun is rising over horizon).

Snack

1) Snap right hand at chest level.
2) Changes to "G" hand at mouth.

Lunch

ASL sign

Right "L" hand moves in
a circular motion at
corner of mouth.

1) Right "O" hand makes eating
motion in front of mouth.
2) Left "B" hand, palm in rests on
inside of right forearm.
Right "B" hand is straight up.

Dinner

Right "D" hand moves
in a circular motion at
corner of mouth.

ASL sign

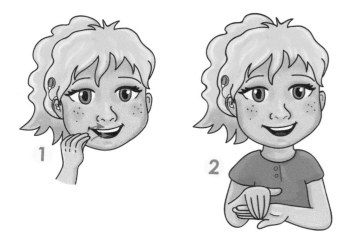

1) Right "O" hand makes eating
motion in front of mouth.
2) At chest level right hand arcs
over left hand (as if sun is setting).

Dirty

1) Chin rests on right hand, palm down. Wiggle fingers.
2) End in "Y" hand.

2 -y

1 dirt

Diaper

"G" hands on hips. Thumb and index finger pinch and move (as if opening a diaper tab).

Silly

Right "Y" hand shakes in front of eyes.

Bite

Right hand bites left index finger.

Hurt

Tap tips of index fingers together twice.

23

Happy

Right hand at chest level,
palm open, brushes
upwards with fingertips.

Again

Right fingertips arc down
and strike heel of left palm.

The End

"T" hand at chest level rotates from palm in to palm out.

Right "E" hand, palm out, rests on left thumb. "E" hand slides across and down left fingertips.

The End

ASL sign for "End"

"B" hands perpendicular, right above
left. Right hand slides along left until it
"falls off" the fingertips.

About the Author

Stacy Eldred searched for years to find resource books and teaching tutorials for her Deaf/Hard of Hearing daughter. After teaching sign language to toddlers and preschoolers for over 10 years, she decided it was time to create a fun, easy, instructive and interactive way for teachers and parents to SEE (Signing Exact English) and ASL (American Sign Language) to hearing and non-hearing children. Thus Emma and Egor were born.

Stacy resides in Northern Virginia and had been developing her sign language skills for 21 years. Her passion is educating and nurturing the minds of children all over the world. It is her goal to reach as many people as possible through Emma and Egor.

About the Illustrator

Lucía Benito was born in Buenos Aires, Argentina, and has been drawing ever since she can remember. She has illustrated many children's books, as well as material for raising public awareness on environmental and social issues.

She considers herself blessed to be able to work at something she loves and in which she excels. In her own words:

"I truly believe that the greatest joy of being a graphic artist is to witness the happiness of the writer when they see their written words turn into images that had only existed in their imagination."

You can see more of her work at: www.tuolvidastodo.com

CPSIA information can be obtained
at www.ICGtesting.com
Printed in the USA
LVHW071034040520
654960LV00013B/1317